The Story of Flamenca

THE STORY OF FLAMENCA

THIS, THE FIRST EDITION OF THE STORY OF FLAMENCA, CONSISTS OF SEVEN HUNDRED AND FIFTY COPIES OF WHICH THIS IS NUMBER

666

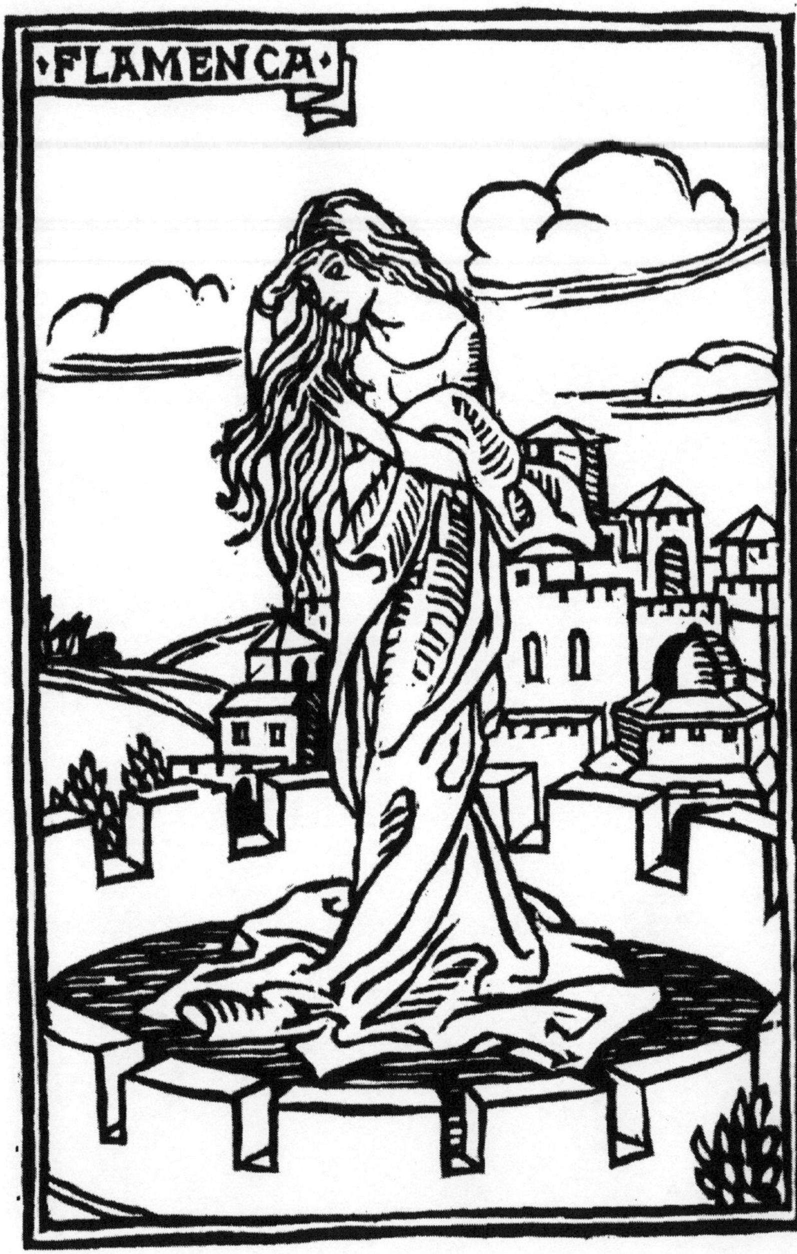
·FLAMENCA·

THE STORY OF FLAMENCA:

The First Modern Novel, Arranged from the Provençal Original of the Thirteenth Century by

WILLIAM ASPENWALL BRADLEY
With WOODCUTS *by* FLORENCE WYMAN IVINS

PUBLISHED IN NEW YORK : : MCMXXII : : BY
HARCOURT, BRACE AND COMPANY

TO J. E. SPINGARN

PREFACE

THE *Roman de Flamenca* occupies a unique place in Provençal literature. "It has," says Meyer, "nothing in common with the old Carolingian and Breton traditions; its subject is not borrowed from the legends transmitted by antiquity to the middle ages; nor would it be possible to see in it one of those popular narratives which are to be found in practically every literature, and whose impersonal character renders it impossible to determine their origin. *Flamenca* is the creation of a man of talent who wished to write an agreeable work representing the most brilliant aspects of courtly life in the twelfth century. It is a novel of manners." [1] As such it has affinities with certain *romans d'aventure*, in the northern idiom, which sim-

[1] *Le Roman de Flamenca*, publié d'après le manuscrit unique de Carcassonne, traduit et accompagné d'un glossaire, par Paul Meyer. Paris, 1865.

ilarly combine a sentimental intrigue with the representation of a particular milieu. *Flamenca*, however, is far superior to any of these in its delicacy, in its verve, in its richness, in the truthful delineation of its characters, and in the bold originality of its conception. Thus it stands alone, not only in Provençal literature, but in medieval literature generally, and may be called, without exaggeration, the first modern novel.

The unique manuscript of *Flamenca* is incomplete. Among the pages missing are the first and last. Hence we have no knowledge of the author or of the date of composition. The latter has been placed approximately in the first half of the thirteenth century. At that time the splendour of the little courts south of the Loire had waned; but the poet shows us the largeness and liberality that had reigned there, while his lightness of tone reflects that relaxing of the old restraints in a sophisticated and pleasure-loving society, which stern moralists would, no doubt, hold responsible for the ensuing swift decadence. Love was the one real religion of the upper classes, and the code of lovers, hardened into a vast, complicated system, constituted the sole effective morality. Flamenca and Guillem are characteristic products of this system, and its perfect exponents. Their acceptance of it is complete. Never does any doubt enter the mind of either as to the sovereignty of the rights conferred by mutual love. Both regard themselves as accomplishing a sacred duty in going directly—or as directly as possible—to the goal of their desire. At the same time, there are forms to observe, and our two lovers are so scrupulous in their observance that they may occasionally seem engaged much more in going through an elaborate ritual than in pursuing dangerously a passionate adventure. Yet the danger was there, and Flamenca never forgets that if, in a sense, she is playing a game, it is a game the stake of which is death.

In my version I have stressed the realistic
elements in order to bring the story into
closer harmony with modern sentiment. Nor
is this the only liberty I have taken. If
Flamenca's virtues are its own, its defects it
shares with nearly all imaginative literature
of the middle ages. It is inordinately long
and lacking in a sense of proportion. The
interest is not sustained throughout and,
after the meeting of the lovers, ceases en-
tirely. Accounts of banquets and fêtes are
interminably protracted, and page after page
is filled with ingeniously subtile discourses
on love. Although the allegorical element
does not dominate here, as in the *Roman de
la Rose*, it begins to rear its head obtrusively,
and there is a marked abuse of dreams and
visions. It is because of these shortcomings
that, despite its charm, it has remained
relatively unknown. Hence I have not
hesitated to operate heroically, cutting to
the bone in many places, and adding a
ligature or two when necessary. Some will,

no doubt, reproach me with the sacrifice of more than one delightful passage; but my purpose throughout has been to disengage the story itself, in its main lines, and anything that interfered with this has had to go.

Wishing to take counsel of Flamenca in my undertaking, I made a pilgrimage last summer to the scene of her suffering and happy release. Alas, I found little at Bourbon-l'Archambault, now an obscure thermal station of the *Centre*, to remind me of my heroine. There are, indeed, on a height dominating the town the romantic ruins of an imposing castle which one would willingly accept as her prison; but my guide informed me that this fortress was not erected till more than a century later, though doubtless it occupies the same site. At the baths, save for a few remains from Roman times, nothing goes farther back than the seventeenth century, when this was one of the favorite resorts of the court. Madame de Montespan is remembered in the name of a hotel which,

for all I know, replaces the comfortable es-
tablishment of the complaisant Pierre Gui;
but not the slightest construction of any sort
evokes the memory of the real lady of Bourbon.

It was only when I reached the church,
situated on a green knoll outside the town,
that I touched a little of that remote past.
Though the venerable edifice has been much
restored, parts of it may well have been
standing in Flamenca's time. The interior
is degraded by the grossest modern poly-
chroming, but I remarked certain capitals
which belong to the earliest period of Gothic
sculpture. One, representing gnome-like
musicians playing curious instruments, wind
and string, brought irresistibly back the de-
scription of Flamenca's wedding feast, when
"harpers harped, fifers fifed . . . and all
performed so well that a great uproar reigned
in the hall." Placing myself in the choir,
as nearly as possible where, it seemed to me,
Guillem must have stood when he heard

mass there for the first time, I too waited for Flamenca to appear. It was, no doubt, one of those lesser feasts, "for which Flamenca would no more have set foot out of doors than for that of a simple martyr not in the calendar"; for I waited in vain. Never a glint of her golden hair crossed the threshold. So I was obliged to leave Bourbon-l'Archambault no richer than I had gone there, and finish my little book without her aid.

W. A. B.

Paris, May, 1922.

THE STORY OF FLAMENCA

THE STORY OF FLAMENCA

I

COUNT Guy of Nemours had a daughter, Flamenca, whose beauty was such that the fame of it passed into every land, and all who heard thereof would fain have her for wife. Many sent messengers to make their suit: knights, nobles, and even the Slav king, who offered to ally himself with the count and aid him against his enemies.

But Guy, who loved his daughter, did not wish her to depart so far thence.

"I would rather," he said, "she were a simple chatelaine, and see her each week or month or even year, than a queen and lose her forever."

Thus, in the end, he made choice of Archambaut, lord of Bourbon, whose friendship he had long sought, and than whom no better knight girded on sword from there to the end of the world

Now when Archambaut heard these tidings, how the count would have him for son, and none other; and when he learned, too, from his messengers, that the hundredth part had not been told him of the damsel's beauty, he rejoiced greatly and set out with a fair following of one hundred knights and four hundred squires, all mounted, for Nemours.

He arrived there three days before the time appointed for his wedding, and when he saw Flamenca he felt his heart inflamed, all flooded over with a sweet amorous fire. Trembling without, he burned within; and though that of which he suffered was not a fever, yet might it have proved fatal, had he not found for it a speedy cure.

Three nights he did not sleep, and Sunday morning he was already clad and shod betimes when the count, entering his room, gave him good morrow from Flamenca.

"Come," he said, "if you would see the damsel in her bower."

Then he took Archambaut by the hand, and led him to Flamenca, who was no whit confused, but only a little blushing.

"Here is your bride, lord Archambaut," said the count. "Take her if you will."

"Sir," he answered, "if there be no hindrance in her, never took I aught so willingly."

Then the damsel, smiling, said to her father:

"Sir, you show clearly you hold me in your power, who dispose of me so lightly. But, since it is your will, I consent."

At this word, "consent," Archambaut felt such joy that he could not keep from taking her hand and pressing it.

Thereupon they departed. Archambaut

knew right well with whom he had left the heart he bore not back with him again. Without once quitting the damsel with his eyes, he drew towards the door, where he bade her farewell. Nor was Flamenca disdainful, but smiled at him and repeated graciously: "God keep you."

Five bishops and ten abbotts, in their robes, awaited them in the church, to marry them. When they had done this and said mass, all went to partake of the feast that had been prepared. Lord Archambaut and the count served at this feast; but the eyes of the first wandered oft to where his heart was, and, could he have had his way, he would have bidden the guests arise from the table before they had half fed.

When the feast was finished and the table was cleared, the jongleurs began. Some sang, others played. All this was a sore trial for lord Archambaut and, had not the night made him amends, I think that neither by food nor by drink, would his life ever have been restored.

The feast lasted more than eight days. Lord Archambaut was happy, for he now had what he most desired, nor was he beset by other care than to serve her whom he wished to honor and please. Had it not been for manly shame which restrained him, he would fain have tired her and handed her himself her gown, her comb, and her mirror.

When, at length, he saw the feast was drawing to a close, and it would ill beseem him to stay longer, he took his leave and set out straight for Bourbon, to prepare his own feast, which he wished to make of such surpassing splendour that the other would no longer be spoken of.

He sent messengers to the king of France, pressing him to come and bring his queen with him. He bade them say to the king that, if he would deign to pass by Nemours, and lead with him the lady Flamenca, he would be his forever.

Then Archambaut caused the city to be decked, and the streets hung with banners and fine tapestries, with silk and with samite. Gold, silver, clothes, and all things else were, by his order, brought together to be given freely to whoever might deign to accept them.

Five hundred suits of raiment, of purple and fine gold, a thousand lances and a thousand shields, a thousand spears and a thousand coats of mail, were made ready in the armory, and a thousand steeds were held waiting in their stalls, for those whom lord Archambaut would make knights.

The king came with a great array, and led Flamenca with him. More than six leagues, more than seven, reached the great company; and, before all the rest, rode the count's son, Flamenca's brother. For he wished to be the first to greet Archambaut, who rode forth to the encounter right well attended with a thousand knights, a thousand burghers, and a thousand varlets.

Each welcomed the king and besought him to lodge with him. He refused saying:

"You press me in vain, for I have the lady Flamenca in my keeping; but my barons will gladly make their abode with you."

So, at the end, all were lodged, and no man kept his door closed. The queen had a good pavillion, and Flamenca was her neighbour.

At the ninth hour all went to meat, and took with them good appetites. Fish of every sort was served, and whatever else is fitting for fast-days, including the fruits that are in season in the month of June, both pears and cherries. The king sent a present of two pieces of agate to Flamenca, who thanked him graciously when the repast was over.

The next day was the feast of Saint John, and it was not permitted to pass without due observance. The bishop of Cleremont

said high mass and preached a sermon on
Our Lord, how He loved Saint John so well
He called him more than prophet. Then
a herald proclaimed, in the king's name,
that none should leave the court before
a fortnight, for any reason, however
weighty.

When they had heard mass, the king spoke
with Flamenca, and led her from the church.
After him followed full three thousand
knights, each leading a lady.

Together they went to the great hall
where the feast was spread. When they had
washed their hands, they were seated, not
on bare benches, but on cushions covered
with cloth; and the napkins on which they
dried their hands were not coarse and rough,
but fine and soft to the touch.

The guests were served with all manner
of meats. Each had what he most liked, and
so much that he who had least had no
reason to envy him who had more. Yet
there were above five hundred who gazed

with wonder upon Flamenca and who, while
they fed their eyes upon her fair face, let
their mouths go hungry.

No one there could compare with Flamenca. For, just as the sun is supreme by
virtue of his splendour, so did she take rank
above all the other ladies by reason of her
beauty. Her color was so fresh, her look
so gentle and gracious, her discourse so wise
and so witty, that the noblest and liveliest
among them remained as if dumb and deem-
ing herself vanquished. They said that one
would strive in vain to appear beautiful by
the side of this lady. And, when they
praised her, you may believe she was indeed
fair; for, in all the world, there are not three
to whom the others will accord beauty, and
praise it.

When all had eaten they again washed
their hands, but remained seated where they
were, and partook of the wine; for such
was the custom in those days. The cloths
being removed, great mirrors—those good

counsellors!—were brought and placed on
tall standards before the guests, so that
each might arrange his dress according to
his liking. Then the jongleurs arose, each
wishing to make himself heard.

He who knew a new piece for the viol,
a song, a lai, or a descant, did his best to
prevail above the others. Harpers harped,
fifers fifed. Some sang the words, while
their fellows played the notes. Both did
their best and all performed so well that a
great uproar reigned in the hall.

Then the king said:

"Sir knights, when the squires have eaten,
cause your steeds to be saddled, and we
shall go to the jousting. While we wait,
I would have the queen lead one dance with
Flamenca, and I too will dance, with the
others."

Thereupon knights, ladies, and damsels
took one another by the hand. Never, in
France or in Brittany, had been seen a
dance so splendid. Two hundred jongleurs,

good players of the viol, took their places in pairs on the benches, and ran the sets without missing a note.

Now the squires had saddled and decked and led around the chargers. When these were seen, the dancing ceased, for never was so brave a sight. Each knight had his squire bring him his arms. Nor did the ladies depart thence, but stayed and found for themselves places in the windows to look out upon those who battled for their sake.

As for lord Archambaut, he lost no time but, with his own hand, dubbed nine hundred and ninety-seven knights, who went forthwith on foot to the palace in silken shoon and presented themselves to the king. He, for handsel, gave them this wish, that they should suffer no greater pain than love might give them. And the queen said likewise.

This day the king himself bore arms. At the tip of his lance he had fastened a sleeve. The queen gave no sign that she was displeased by this token, but she said to herself that, if she knew who had given it to the king, she would make her rue the favor she had bestowed. In her heart she believed it was Flamenca and sent for lord Archambaut, who presented himself fully armed before her.

"My lord," said she, taking him by the hand and seating him beside her in the window, "I am ill at ease and need your counsel."

"Your highness," returned he, "may God keep you."

Then the queen, touching Flamenca, seated nearbye, said:

"My lady, I would speak alone with lord Archambaut."

"Willingly, madam, since you wish it," replied Flamenca.

At the next window sat the countess of Nevers who, when she saw Flamenca draw near, greeted her and made her a cushion of her own mantle. Flamenca, thanking her, sat down beside her, and looked out upon the jousting.

The queen lost no time but broke forth in bitter rage:

"My lord Archambaut, is it not most unseemly for the king to wear thus, beneath my very eyes, an amorous devise? Methinks it is an affront to you, no less than to me."

Archambaut saw clearly that she suspected Flamenca of having given the sleeve to the king.

"By Christ, my lady," he hastened to answer, "I can not see that the king dishonours either you or me in thus bearing the badge of love. With him it is but knightly duty."

"My lord, that is an excuse of which you yourself will have good need before another fortnight be past."

"Nay, madam, seek not to make me jealous where there is no need."

"Do you think then," demanded the

queen, frowning, "that you too will not feel
the pangs of jealousy? By my faith, that
you shall, and not, perchance, without good
cause."

At that moment a jongleur drew near
Archambaut and addressed him, saying:

"Sir, the king desires to bestow arms upon
Thibaut, count of Blois, and I come from
Thibaut himself, who prays you to join
him."

Lord Archambaut took his leave of the
queen more troubled than he let her see.
He was, indeed, in a bad humour because of
what she had said; and, when he had seen
Thibaut and more than four hundred others
knighted by the king, he summoned his
squire:

"Have the bells rung for vespers," he
ordered. "It will be time to sup when the
king has heard them."

When the ladies, seated at the windows,
heard the bells, they cried:

"Why, it is not yet none, and already

they are ringing vespers! May she lose her
husband who stirs a step while yet one
knight is left in the lists! Never shall I
leave the tiltyard for vespers!"

The king entered at that moment and,
going graciously up to Flamenca, led her
away. The barons followed him and led
the ladies to church. When the office was
ended, the king brought Flamenca back
and playfully placed his hand upon her
breast.

The queen was very wroth at this, and
lord Archambaut also, though he gave no
sign.

Then they supped. The tables were furnished with roast meats, with fruits, with
fresh roses and violets, and with snow and
ice to cool the wine, that it might not banish
sleep. All were tired with the diversions of
this day, and soon went to seek repose till
the morrow.

The next morning, at daybreak, the new-
made knights, clad in their gear, rode through

the streets, ringing bells of every sort.
They made a fine hubbub, and Archambaut's
trouble grew as he heard it. In his heart
was such grief he was like to die thereof.
Yet he sought to hold himself in leash,
blaming the queen for the suspicions she
had sown in his breast, and concealing his
feelings from the others.

Nineteen days the feast lasted, and all
marvelled whence Archambaut could draw
the great treasure he gave in largesse. On
the twentieth day the king and queen took
their departure; for the queen did not wish
the feast to last the full month, now that
she believed the king to be in love with
Flamenca; but the king did not love with
real love, and thought only to honor lord
Archambaut when, in the presence of his
host, he embraced Flamenca, and kissed her.

Archambaut set his guests upon their way
right courteously, but his heart was gnawed
by sharp jealous pangs. As he rode back,
he raved wildly and, when he had returned,

his companions left him, thinking he had lost his senses. Alone, he cried:

"Alas, of what was I thinking when I took unto myself a wife! Good God, I was mad. Had I not everything I needed to make me happy? A curse on my friends and family who counselled me that which is ever for men a source of sorrow. Now, indeed, I have a wife; but much good does she do me, who consumes me with jealousy."

Lord Archambaut was in an evil case. Leaving all his affairs in disorder, he made great dole when anyone came to the castle, and could hardly keep from throwing him out head-first. In every visitor he feared a rival. If one so much as spoke to his wife, he thought to see her ravished before his eyes.

"That is how all this came to pass. The king chose well his moment. Even before they left Nemours I believe he essayed her. I thought I had naught to fear from him, or I should have known how to guard her against his devices. Now as many as wish can come and go, and there are never enough for her liking.

"Mark the welcome she gives them! She shows clearly she is no longer mine. Alas, unhappy wretch that I am! Cursed be the hour wherein I was born! The queen knew well what she was saying, when she told me I would be jealous. Curses on her, too, prophetess of evil!"

Then he broke into a great rage, tearing his hair, biting his lips, gnashing his teeth, and glaring fiercely at Flamenca. Scarce could he keep from cutting off her gleaming golden tresses.

"My lord, what ails you?" she asked him.

"What! Christ! I die, and you mock me! This is the work of these brave gallants who come to see you; but, by my faith, they will no longer find the way open to you. He who takes a wife has his trouble for naught if he put her not in some safe place and keep guard over her. This shall I do. The tower is high, the wall is wide, and here you shall stay with only your damsels to keep you company."

He delayed not, but, sending for a mason, led him straight to Flamenca's tower. There he ordered him to cut a window into the kitchen, that her food might be passed through to her, and that he himself might spy upon his wife the more easily.

The sweet child now knew not what to do. Her life henceforth was little better than death. If her days were bad, her nights were worse, holding naught for her but weariness. She had to wait upon her two pretty maids, whose sorrows equalled hers, for they too were prisoners. Gentle and kind, they did what they could to comfort their mistress, and thinking only of the love they bore her, they forgot their own pain. The name of one of these damsels was Alis, of the other, Margarida.

God sent great grief unto Flamenca. Many sighs and much agony of heart were hers because of her husband, and she shed bitter tears, being filled with sadness and affliction. Yet one signal mark of grace He bestowed upon her that, having no child, He put not love into her heart. For, loving, and having naught whereon to nourish her love, she would have suffered more sorely.

Long time she lived thus afflicted, never passing the door save on Sundays and feast days. Even in church neither knight nor clerk could speak with her. For Archambaut kept her ever in a dark corner behind a wide screen he had built to the level of her chin. He did not let her go to the altar for Communion, but made the priest bring the offering, which he gave her himself. A little clerk gave her the pax, and he, at least, might have got a glimpse of her, had he but known how to manage it.

After the words: *Ite missa est*, Archambaut left without waiting for sixte or none.

"Come, come," he said to the young women, "Let me dine at once. Do not keep me waiting."

He did not even give them time to say their prayers.

Thus passed two years. Every day the poor prisoners saw their pain redoubled, while Archambaut swore and groaned and guarded them both morning and night.

II

Now at this time, while Archambaut was thus jealous and, in all Auvergne, songs, sirventes, couplets, and sonnets were made upon him, there dwelt in Burgundy a knight whom Nature had delighted to fashion and instruct. Nor had she failed in this task, for never has been seen a youth so fair of person or of goodlier mien.

He had light curling hair, broad white forehead, dark arching brows, black laughing eyes, and nose as straight as the stock of an arbalest. His shoulders were broad, his muscles strong. When he jousted, none could sustain the shock of his assault. Lifting his foe from the saddle, he passed on bearing him at the end of his lance.

He had studied at Paris and learned there so much of the seven arts that he could have taught school anywhere. He could both read and write, and spoke English better than any clerk. His name was Guillem de Nevers.

Guillem was at all points a good knight. He led a fair following to the tourney, took captives and made prizes. What he thus won he spent and gave away freely in presents. He loved gaming, dogs, falcons—all pleasant things, in short, and suited to his estate. One only he lacked, and that was any experience of love.

He had read all the poets who treat thereof and instruct lovers. From them he had learned that, without love, one could not lead the life ordained for noble youth, and often he dreamed of engaging in some high adventure that would bring him both pleasure and honour.

Thus it happened that, when Guillem heard how Flamenca was held prisoner by her jealous husband, his heart spoke, and said to him that, were he but able to speak with her, he might, perchance, enjoy her love.

Long he pondered upon this. Then, one night, Love appearing in a dream, urged him to the adventure and made him fair promises. Next day Guillem set forth, with his companions, for Bourbon.

Now there were baths at Bourbon in those days, where all could come and bathe at their ease. A tablet in each bath made known the properties of the water both hot and cold, that sprang from two spouts, and over it was built a house, with quiet rooms wherein to take one's ease.

Of these baths the best were those belonging to Pierre Gui, a right honest man who was on terms of amity with lord Archambaut; and when Guillem, arriving at Bourbon, demanded where he might lodge, he was directed thither.

The goodman, seated at the door of his hostel, seeing the youth approach, arose and greeted him graciously, while his wife, Dame Bellapila, invited him within and gave him his dinner. When he had eaten, Pierre Gui showed him his rooms and gave him free choice among them.

Guillem wanted one thing only, which was to be so lodged that he could see Flamenca's tower from his window. When he had found this, he said, dissembling:

"This room pleases me, because it is larger than the others, and of a more agreeable aspect."

"As you like," replied his host. "Here you will be undisturbed, and master of all you do. Count Raoul often makes this room his abode when he comes to Bourbon; but it is a long time since he has shown himself here. For our master, who was so good a knight, is sadly changed. Since he took him a wife, he has not laced helm or donned hauberk, and he holds the world as naught.

I doubt not, however, you have heard these things reported of him."

"I have, indeed, heard them spoken of," replied Guillem, "but I have far other concerns. I suffer from a sore ailment, and if the waters here heal me not, I know not what I shall do to be cured."

"Rest assured as to that, fair sir," answered Pierre Gui. "Know that no one, however sick, comes to our baths without going away cured, if only he stay long enough."

The room was large and clean and well furnished. There wanted neither bed nor hearth nor aught else for comfort. Guillem caused all his belongings to be brought and placed therein. Then, when his host had retired, he dismissed his squires, instructing them to let none know his name, saying simply that he was from Besançon.

It was the night after Easter, the season when the nightingale accuses with his songs those who have no care of love. One sang in the grove near Guillem's window, and the young man could not close his eyes, though his couch was white and soft and wide.

"Ah Love," he sighed, "what will become of me? At your behest, leaving my own people, I have come into this country a pilgrim, a stranger. Sighing without cease, I suffer from a desire that has taken fast hold of my heat. I feign sickness now, it is true; but I shall need to feign it no longer, if I am not soon cured of this ill."

Then, as day was beginning to break, and his bed brought him no repose, he arose, crossed himself, and prayed to Saint Blaise, Saint Martin, Saint George, Saint Genies, and five or six other saints who were gentle knights, that they might make intercession for him. Before beginning to dress, he opened his window and looked upon the tower where his lady languished.

"O lady tower," he cried, "you are beautiful without and pure and white within. Would to God I were inside your walls, so as not to be seen of Archambaut, of Margarida, or of Alis!"

So saying, his arms fell, his feet no longer sustained him, his color fled, and he fainted. One of his squires, seeing him about to fall, seized him, held him close, and bore him to the bed. The squire was greatly frightened, for he could not feel the beat of his master's heart. This was because Love had transported his spirit to Flamenca's tower, where Guillem held her in his arms, and caressed her so gently she was not aware of it. Then his soul, having had its will, returned to his body, which was not long in reviving.

It was clear he had come back from a place full of delight, for he was more blithe and beautiful than before. The young squire had wept so much that his master's face was wet with his tears.

"Sir," he said, drying his eyes, "I have been sore troubled."

"Ah, my friend," sighed Guillem, "your concern was occasioned by my happiness."

Clad in breeches and shirt, he took his place once more in the window, throwing over his shoulders a mantle of vair trimmed with gris. The tower stood to the right, and naught could turn Guillem from it, while putting on his shoes—elegant buskins fashioned at Douai.

He called for his ewer. Then, when he had washed, he laced up his sleeves with a silver bodkin. Over all he passed a cape of black silk, and studied carefully the figure he made.

As he was thus occupied, his host entered to lead him to the church. There Guillem, kneeling at the altar of Saint Clement, prayed devoutly to God, as also to Mary, to Michael, and to all the saints, to aid him. Then, taking a psalter, he opened it. Straight way he came upon a verse which filled him with delight: "Dilexi quoniam."

"God knows well what I desire," he exclaimed, closing the book. He made careful note of the place where his lady would sit, and prayed that naught might keep her from coming.

When it was time for mass, Guillem took his place, with his host, in the choir, where he could look out through a little opening, without being seen. His heart beat loudly as he awaited the arrival of Flamenca; and, at each shadow that fell across the doorway, he thought Archambaut was about to enter.

Everyone else had arrived, and the third bell had rung, when the jealous husband, uncouth and unkempt, entered the church. Beside him, but keeping well her distance, for it was clear he filled her with disgust, came Flamenca.

She paused an instant on the threshold, to make her reverence, and then it was, for the first time, that Guillem saw his lady. He ceased to gaze upon her only when she passed behind her screen. Then he knelt with the others.

"Asperges me," proclaimed the priest. Guillem took up the response at the

"Domine," and sang it clear through. Never before had it been so well sung in that church.

The priest left the choir, followed by a clerk bearing the holy water. When he came to Flamenca, he did his best to spray her across the screen, and she uncovered a little her hair, where it was parted in the middle, the better to receive the water on her forehead. Her skin showed white and fine, and the golden crown of her hair, where the sun chanced to strike it with one of his rays, at that instant, shone resplendent. At the sight of this splendid sample of what love held in store for him, Guillem trembled with joy, and intoned the "Signum salutis."

The priest then returned to the altar and said the "Confiteor," with his little clerk. At the Evangel, Flamenca arose. At first a burgher, to Guillem's disgust, stood in front of her; but God willed him to move to one side, that she might be seen unobscured. To cross herself, she lowered a little the band which covered her mouth and chin, and with one finger loosened the latchets of her mantle. Guillem gazed at her bare hand which seemed to steal his heart from his breast and bear it away. The emotion which seized him was so strong that he was like to faint of it.

By good fortune, he found at his feet a stool on which to kneel, as if in prayer. He stayed thus, quite still, till the little clerk gave him the pax. When, in her turn, Flamenca kissed the breviary, Guillem saw, for a moment, her red mouth, and the sight filled him with sweet joy.

When the clerk had finished giving the pax, Guillem considered how he might gain possession of the book.

"My friend," he whispered to the clerk, "have you a calendar? I wish to learn on what day falls Pentecost."

The youth handed him the book, but Guillem gave small heed to the day of the month or the year. He turned the leaves from end to end, and would fain have kissed them all for the sake of one, could he have done so without being remarked.

"Clerk," he asked, "where is it that you give the pax? Is it not in the psalter?"

"Here is the place, sir," the clerk answered, and showed it to Guillem who, kneeling again as if in prayer, kissed the page more than a thousand times, and did not cease from his devotions till the priest had said: "Ite missa."

Archambaut left the church without delay, forcing Flamenca to follow with her damsels. Guillem waited for the priest to finish none, then addressed him courteously:

"Sir," he said, 'I demand a boon. Dine with me today at my hostel, and hereafter, as long as I stay, be my guest at table."

The priest consented gladly, and all three repaired at once to the hostel, where dinner awaited them.

When they had finished and the table was cleared, Guillem sent one of his squires to fetch the gifts he had designed for his host and hostess. To the former he gave a long belt with a buckle of French make, worth more than a silver mark; to the latter, a piece of stuff to fashion a summer mantle. So grateful were they for these gifts that they promised to do all in their power to serve Guillem. They even offered to move out of their house and leave it all to him, should he so desire.

He accepted gladly. Then, turning to the priest, Dom Justin, he said: "I ask you now to cut the hair from the top of my head, and make me a tonsure such as I had before. I am a canon of Péronne, and would return now to that estate."

The priest could scarce answer at first, so surprised was he at Guillem's request; but, while the others wept to see the young man thus despoiled of his golden crown, the little clerk, whose name was Nicholas, held the basin, and Dom Justin shore off the locks with sharp shears, clipping the hair close about the neck, and making a large tonsure.

Guillem gave the priest a gilded goblet, worth four marks, as his reward.

"The barber," said he, "must be well paid."

"My lord, it is too much!" protested the priest. "Tell me what I can do to merit more fully so rich a gift."

"Take me for your clerk," said Guillem. "As for Nicholas, here, send him to Paris to study. He is not yet too old, and he will learn more in two years there than here in three. I will give him four golden marks a year, and furnish him with raiment."

"My lord, blessed be the day we first met," cried the priest. "Nothing has so pained me as to see my nephew losing time precious for his studies. Already he can write and make verses, and when he has studied two years he will know twice as much. As for your request, you shall be master, and I will do all you desire."

"Nay," exclaimed Guillem hastily, "you must give me your promise to treat me in all ways as your little clerk. Else I shall

fail of my purpose, which is to serve humbly
both you and God at the same time."

Then he instructed the priest to have
fashioned for him a large round cape of
brown silk or garbardine, which should
cover him from head to foot.

"I no longer wish to follow the fêtes of
the court," he said, "for all that is but derision
and vain smoke; and he who thinks to have
gained most from it, finds himself poorest
when night falls."

Thus preached Isengrin. Had the priest
been wilier he might have said, with Renard:
"You are hiding your real game." But he
suspected nothing, and went out with the
squires to order the cape.

Next morning, after mass, Guillem went
to the baths. There he examined carefully
the soil, and found it was of tufa so soft he
could cut it with a knife. That very after-
noon, when his hosts had moved out, he sent
to Chatillon secretly for some laborers.

Saturday Nicholas left, and Guillem assisted at vespers. At first he held his cape a little high, for he was forever placing his hand upon his hip, as had been his habit; but he played his part well, and Dom Justin was overjoyed at having such a clerk sent him by heaven.

After vespers Guillem went over with the priest the lessons and responses for the next morning.

That night he did not sleep. At the first stroke of the bell for matins, he arose and ran to the church, where, seizing the rope from the hands of the priest, he finished ringing lustily.

After matins Dom Justin told Guillem he might rest a little, and led him to a room, next the belfry, which had belonged to Nicholas; but, though the floor was strewn with reeds and rushes, he could not close his eyes, for now a new care assailed him. What should he say to his lady, when he gave her the pax?

Long he lay and pondered, calling on Love

to aid him at this pass. At last, finding naught, he arose and went out, closing the door and putting the key on the shelf, whence Dom Justin had taken it. Then he requested a beadle, one Vidal, to bring him the salt for the holy water. While mixing this, the priest awoke, and Guillem gave him some of the water to wash. Then they began prime.

When they had sung tierce and rung again, the people began to come for mass. After the main body, as usual, arrived Archambaut, followed by Flamenca, who passed behind her screen.

Seeing her, Guillem had eyes for naught else. He did not, however, neglect his duties. As he had the offices by heart, these were easy for him. His voice was fresh and clear, and rang out as he sang the "Agnus Dei." Then he took the book and offered it to his host, who sat in the choir. Pierre Gui passed it to those without, and the pax proceeded thus through the church.

Guillem followed the book as it went from hand to hand; but he moved so slowly through the press that Archambaut had already received the pax, by the time he reached the little cell that held his treasure. Trembling, without daring to look up, he drew near, fully resolved to say at least a word, yet not knowing, even now, what it would be. With a prayer to Love to aid him, he approached, and as Flamenca kissed the psalter, he murmured: "Alas!" then withdrew, his head humbly bowed. Had he disarmed a hundred knights in a tourney, he would have been less happy.

His joy was great, but of brief duration. It lasted while he folded up the altar cloths and put away safely the chalice and the paten; but, when he was alone in his room once more, he was all despair.

"Alas," he cried, "I deserve to die. Love, thou hast been of slight aid to me. I thought to throw a six, and I have come off with an ace. Never in this world could my lady have

heard me. Else she would at least have
lifted her eyes, nor so soon drawn back behind her screen. It was her wimple betrayed
me, that covered her ears so closely. Curses
on the father of such a fashion!"

Flamenca, however, had not failed to hear
Guillem's "alas," and suffered some despite
from it. She showed no sign while Archambaut was with her; but, when he went out
after dinner, she gave way to her grief.

"It would have been for me, rather, to cry
'alas!'" she made moan. "He suffers not,
being neither sick nor in prison. Why then
insult my sufferings? Dear God, what harm
have I done him, that he should assail me
in such a place?"

"Come hither, sweet children," she cried
to Alis and Margarida, "and give heed to
what is troubling me. A young man I know
not, whose face I have never seen before, has
basely insulted me."

"What young man, my lady?" demanded
Margarida.

"He who gave me the pax."

"What did he say, madam?" asked Alis.

"I will tell you, though it pains me even to recall it. To mock and torment me, in handing me the psalter, he murmured 'alas!' as if it were he who suffered, not I."

"What was his bearing, my lady, as he said this?"

"He kept his eyes cast down."

"Why, then, madam, I am not so sure he meant to insult you. It appears to me as if he felt some fear in your presence, rather than overweening pride."

"It is true," reflected Flamenca, that "he blushed and sighed."

"Certainly," then broke in Alis, "this young man did not seem so ill-bred as to wish to harm you. Besides, he is not the one who always gives us the pax. He is taller and handsomer. He is more skilled at reading, also, and sings more clearly. In short, he had all the seeming of a gentleman."

"My lady," spoke up Margarida, once

more, "I do not know this young man, or what he wants of you, but I think you would do well to discover his meaning."

"You speak as if that were an easy matter," replied Flamenca, petulantly. "How can I?"

"Christ, my lady," exclaimed Alis, "if it were left to me, I should manage easily enough. Ask him! He said 'alas'. Do you say to him now: 'Why do you complain?'"

"I can try," said Flamenca, still doubtful.

So the following Sunday, when Guillem gave her the pax, she took the psalter and, tilting it a trifle towards Archambaut, she whispered: "Why do you complain?"

It was Flamenca's turn now to be troubled and to ask if Guillem had heard her.

"Did you hear me, Alis?" she demanded when they had returned from church.

"Not I, madam."

"And you, Margarida?"

"No, my lady, I heard nothing. How did

you speak? Show us, and we shall be able to tell you if he heard."

"Stand up, Alis," commanded Flamenca, "and pretend you are giving me the pax. Take that copy of *Blanchefleur* for the breviary."

Alis jumped up, ran to the table where the book lay, and came back to her mistress, who, for all her sadness, could scarce keep from laughing at the sight of the young girl counterfeiting the clerk. Then Flamenca, tilting the book a trifle, as in the church, and pretending to kiss it, said: "Why do you complain?"

"There, did you hear me?" she asked eagerly.

"Yes indeed," they both cried. "If you spoke like that, there can be no doubt."

Next week, Guillem, this time having prepared his answer, came straight towards his lady, who loosened her wimple that she might hear the more clearly. As she took the pax, he said: "I die."

"Nay, he must not die, my lady!" cried Margarida, when Flamenca had repeated this response. "I swear I have never seen so handsome a young clerk."

"What can I do?" asked her mistress, weakly.

"Ask him: 'Of what?' since that is what we wish to know."

This same Sunday the workmen came from Chatillon. They marvelled greatly at the oath Guillem required of them before making known the task they were to accomplish. This was to dig a passage under the ground between the baths and his own room. They were skilful and worked rapidly, in such wise that in short space the passage was completed and so cunningly contrived at both ends that not a sign of it showed.

When, on the eighth day, Guillem gave the pax, Flamenca whispered: "Of what?" then drew back quickly.

"My little Margarida, I said it," she exclaimed when they were back in the tower.

"Thank God for that, my lady! I only hope he heard you this time, too."

"You may set your mind at rest, my dear. He moved away so slowly that he could not have helped hearing me. Now we shall know the answer on Thursday, for that is the feast of the Ascension."

"Madam, methinks these feasts come far less often now than at any other season," pouted Alis. "The rest of the year, when we have no need of them, there is one nearly every day. While here, this summer, we have had five full weeks with nothing but Sundays!"

On his side, Guillem repeated Flamenca's question and pondered it.

"'Of what?' she asked me. Well, it will not be hard to tell her that, for I know only too well whereof I suffer."

Thursday, therefore, at tierce, he said: "Of love."

That night Flamenca lay on her bed, more pensive than ever, and with something resembling distress at her heart.

"Well, what did he say, my lady?" asked Alis at last.

"Ah, my friend, you could never guess. It is quite different from anything we might have imagined. He says it is love of which he suffers. Did anyone ever hear of a stranger coming thus to complain of love?"

"Faith, madam," laughed Alis, with a sly look at Margarida, "of what evil did you think he came here to complain? Surely, had he been beaten or robbed, he would not have sought to lay his complaint before you."

"But for whom is this love? pursued Flamenca, still puzzled.

"Why my lady, I can guess readily enough," replied Margarida, also laughing; "but since you would have sure knowledge, ask him that, too."

"Good God! Is it a jest?" cried Guillem on Sunday, when she had asked him: "For whom?" "Is it possible she does not suspect my love? How can she help knowing that I love her with all my heart? But, since she asks me, I will gladly tell her."

So on the day of Pentecost, Guillem, trembling, answered: "For you."

Then was Flamenca sore troubled.

"What!" she exclaimed. "Can it be for me he cherishes an amorous desire? Then he must needs seek another mistress, for my love is no love at all, but sorrow and anguish. Sobs and sighs, troubles and tears, bitterness and sadness of heart—these are my near neighbors, my privy companions. What shall I do, what shall I say?"

"My lady," exclaimed Margarida, "whatever you do or say, you will surely not let that gallant young man love you and entreat you in vain! Who knows but God Himself has sent him to deliver you from prison?"

"Even were I to return his love, I do not

see how that would advantage him in aught," said Flamenca.

"Ask him, my lady. He has done so well already, he will surely know."

So, the following Sunday Flamenca said: "What can I do?" and the eighth day after Pentecost, on the feast of Saint Barnaby—a little feast for which Flamenca would no more have set foot out of doors than for that of a simple martyr not in the calendar—Guillem answered "Cure."

"How can I cure his ills, who am without remedy for my own?" pondered Flamenca, and her damsels counselled her to ask: "How?"

"Trust him. He will easily find a way to compass your happiness at the same time as his own."

"May God in His mercy will it so," sighed Flamenca, "for at present I do not see how we shall ever be able to do more for each other than we do now."

"In little space God works," replied Alis

devoutly, "and brave effort overcomes all obstacles."

The following Sunday was the feast of Saint John. It was not a day lost for Guillem, whose lady, in taking the psalter, and whispering: "How?" brushed his finger with her hand. When he was alone again, he sang for joy.

"O God," he cried, "I swear by the apostles and the prophets, I will give all my rents from France for the building of churches and bridges, if you will but let me see my lady face to face!"

The next time, drawing near with a high heart, he said: "I have found a way!"

"He has already found a way!" exclaimed Alis, gleefully. "Were this the olden time, lady dear, and there came such a friend to me, I should think 'twas Jupiter or some other God, who was in love with me. Answer him boldly, then: "Take it."

Flamenca sighed, her colour came and

went, she still hesitated. Suddenly Alis sneezed.

"Bless you!" the damsel exclaimed. "Now everything is bound to come out right. We could not have a better omen."

"God bless you both," cried Flamenca, deeply touched, "for all the hope and courage you have given me. I will do as you say, though I know not if, in thus accepting his love so readily, I shall not be dishonoured."

"My Lady," Alis assured her, "there can be no dishonour, since Love wills it so."

Thursday was the feast of the passion of the two glorious apostles, who hold the first place after Saint Michael, in Paradise. That day, then, by her answer, Flamenca confirmed Guillem's every hope. How shall I tell his delight? Now he was sure that Love wished to exalt him above all other lovers, and the next time he said to his lady: "I have taken it." At the same moment their eyes met and their hearts embraced.

"Can it be possible," wondered Flamenca,

"that in three days' time, he has found a way whereby I may heal him? How wanting in faith was I! It was a sin even to doubt him. I promise now, before God, that if he can bring us together, I shall be his, and his alone, forever more."

"Small love do I owe the knights of my country! Two whole years have I dwelt in bitter grief, and not one has given a thought to me. And the knights of this country! Scarcely do they merit the renown of true knighthood, who permit a poor stranger lady to perish thus miserably! But this knight has a right to all my love, who, for my sake, has placed his own life in jeopardy."

So Flamenca hesitated no longer but next time asked him boldly: "What shall I do?" and eight days later Guillem, in his turn, answered: "You will go," but did not say where. So, on the feast of the Magdalen, Flamenca inquired: "Where?" and the day following Guillem said: "To the baths," whereat Flamenca divined he had found some way of coming to her in the baths, and prayed God and His saints that there might not thereby come to her any dishonour.

On Tuesday, which was the feast of Saint James of Compostella, she demanded resolutely: "When?"

Great was Guillem's joy, and it would not have been hard for him to answer at once; but he would rather have let himself be tonsured with a cross like a thief, or branded with a red-hot iron, than speak a word which might have betrayed them.

The fifth day thereafter he replied: "Soon."

Then again was Flamenca sorely distressed.

"Fear, shame and love, draw me in different directions," she cried. "Fear chides me and warns that, if he caught me, my husband would burn me alive. Shame bids me beware of the world's dispraise. Love says, on the other hand, that Fear and Shame have never made a brave heart, and that she can never be called a true lover who, through them, lets herself be turned aside.

"Yet, O Love, how grievous are thy darts! Never could I have guessed that to love meant to suffer so sorely! But, since I am at thy mercy, naught remains for me but to receive thee. Enter then into this dwelling which is thine own. My heart shall be thy chamber. Naught shall avail to oppose thy will, for I belong to thee only.

"And to him who comes to claim that which I hold from thee, as thy vassal, I shall answer, without longer delaying, 'With all my heart!'"

At these words she fell into a swoon and remained without consciousness till Archambaut's return.

"Madam, here is our master," cried Alis, fearful lest her mistress, awaking, might let fall some word to arouse his suspicions. She cried so loudly that Flamenca recovered her senses; but, before opening her eyes, she lay still a moment, to prepare what she should say to her husband.

Archambaut was all disturbed. Bringing water, he dashed it in her face. Then at last, opening her eyes, and looking up, she drew a deep sigh.

"My lady," he inquired anxiously, "what ails you?"

"My lord, a pain at my heart is killing me."

"I believe if you took a little nutmeg every day it would cure you."

"No, sire, the baths alone can bring me any relief. Lead me there on Wednesday, I beseech you."

It did not please lord Archambaut to have his wife go to the baths. He took her there as seldom as possible, and always examined each corner carefully before leaving her, for fear some man might be lurking in the corner; but he could not refuse her now.

"Very well, I am willing," he grumbled,

going out in a bad humour to find Pierre
Gui and to tell him to make ready the
baths.

Tuesday Flamenca, who found herself
well enough to go to the church, said: "With
all my heart," and, with her left hand, lightly
brushed Guillem's right. He returned home
in a state of rapture, and that evening he
heard his host say to two servants:

"Cleanse the baths and empty them so
that they will fill up afresh for our lady, who
will come tomorrow at an early hour."

Wednesday, at daybreak, Flamenca, feign-
ing a return of her malady, made great dole,
as well she might, for she had not slept a
wink. She called feebly to her husband:

"Never in all my life have I suffered as
I do now. Hasten, I beseech you, and be
not too vexed, for you will soon be rid of
me. Indeed, rather would I die than endure
my present pain; and, if the baths restore
me not, already I hold myself to be no better
than one dead."

The damsels were already up and dressed. They went first, taking with them their basins and unguents, while Archambaut followed reluctantly, leading his wife to her lover.

When he had looked well in all the corners, as was his wont, he went out, locking the door. Quickly the damsels sprang to bar it on the inside. Then, looking at each other, they said:

"What shall we do? We know not where or how he will enter, who has given us this tryst."

"I am no wiser than you," replied Flamenca. "I see nothing changed in the appearance of the place. Yet I have no thought to undress, since I did not come here to bathe."

Scarcely had she spoken, when they heard a little noise. The next instant Guillem lifted a stone in the floor, and entered.

In his hand he held a candle. His shirt and his breeches were of fine linen from

Rheims. His shoes were of silk embroidered with flowers. His well-cut doublet was fashioned of some costly stuff, and he wore, on his head, a little cloth cap, sewn with silk. Love had lent him somewhat of his pallor, but he was only the handsomer for that. Kneeling before Flamenca, he said:

"My lady, may He Who created you, and Whose will it is that you should be without peer for beauty and graciousness, save you—you and yours!"

And he bowed low at her feet.

"Fair sir," replied Flamenca, "may He Who never lies and Who willed you to come hither, protect you, and permit you to accomplish all your desire."

"All my desire, sweet lady, all my thought, all my trouble and my pain, are for you, to whom I have given myself. And, if you, in turn, will give yourself to me, all my wishes will be fulfilled."

"Fear not. Since God has granted us to come together, you will have naught to complain of in me.   Besides, since long time, my heart has been yours."

He took her in his arms and kissed her tenderly and embraced her, then said:

"If it be your pleasure, we can seek, by the safe way I have made, the room where I have so often gazed upon your tower."

"As you will, sweet friend.   I shall go whithersoever you lead me, sure that you will bring me back again in all security."

The passage was not dark, for it was lighted with candles, and, before they knew it, they were in the chamber, which was richly furnished with tapestries, with benches, with precious stuffs of all sorts, and strewn with green rushes.

Guillem and Flamenca seated themselves upon a couch raised a little above the level of the floor, while Alis and Margarida took cushions at their feet.

Flamenca looked at them fondly.

"Dear friend," she said, "never have these damsels grown weary in pleading your suit. And, had it not been for their wise counsels and good sense, never would you have had your desire."

Guillem thanked them warmly, begging them to accept of him girdles, diadems, ribbons, bracelets, brooches, rings, little bags of musk, and still other trinkets. Then, turning to Flamenca, he said:

"Sweet love, a boon, I beseech you."

"Name it, dear friend. I think no wish of yours could prove displeasing to me."

"I have two cousins," he answered, "Otho and Clari, who follow me that they, too, one day, may be made knights. It would please me were they to have some share in our happiness."

"How mean you?"

"My squires are young and debonair, like your two damsels, in whose company they would not want whereof to speak. And, if they found it in their hearts to love one another, they would but love us the more."

"It shall be even as you say," assented Flamenca gladly, and Guillem, opening the door, told his squires to enter.

They marvelled greatly at seeing Flamenca, and when their eyes fell upon the two damsels, they believed they were under some spell. Quickly they fell to their knees.

"Here am I, lady, to do your bidding," said each of them in turn.

Flamenca was well pleased, and welcomed the young men graciously. Then, turning to her young women:

"Come hither, both of you," she addressed them. "Here are two young men, and you are two, also. It is my wish that each should have her friend. Wait not to be entreated. 'Tis I, your mistress, who entreat, who tell, who command you, to do all their desire. Go to the baths. Pleasure awaits you there."

Then Alis chose Otho, and Margarida had Clari. Together all four went to the baths, where there were pleasant chambers, from which Alis and Margarida had no need to come forth as they went in, unless they so desired.

When they were alone, Guillem, turning to Flamenca, said:

"Long have I suffered for your sweet sake a martyr's pains. Now that we have come together at last, I thank you for these; but you know not yet who I am, unless it be that Love has told you I am your man."

"My friend," said Flamenca, "I doubt not you are of some high estate. This I know by the knightly soul you have shown in wishing to be my lover."

Then Guillem recounted to her, word by word, who he was, how he had come, and all he had done since he had been at Bourbon.

When Flamenca knew what manner of man her Guillem was, she was so full of joy she gave herself to him without stint. She threw her arms about his neck and kissed him with all her heart.

Many times did they kiss each other on

the eyes and on the mouth and on the hands
and on the neck, and many times did they
do for each other all those things without
which joy in love is incomplete. Each
sought to appease the heavy burden and the
long desire that each for the other had suffered.

They took pleasure too, in rehearsing the
words they had spoken, and so lovely was
their delight, that man would not know how
to record, or mouth to speak, or mind to
conceive it.

When it came time to part, Guillem called
his squires and the damsels. These, their
eyes wet with tears, thanked him for the
happiness that had been theirs in the company of the young men.

Guillem, too, wept when he took leave
of his lady, for it seemed to him he would
never see her more. He was, however, to
see her again, and that many times; for,
henceforth, Flamenca would return to the
baths as often as she pleased.

The season of sorrow and sadness was over at last for this lady and her two damsels. No longer did they remember their prison, or the jealous husband who kept them there in vain; for, from this sad trial, had sprung, for them, joy and happiness.

Lightning Source UK Ltd.
Milton Keynes UK
UKHW010012030119
334668UK00008B/986/P

9 781363 652105